Look Around

Genesis 1 tells us how God created ever...

bread	fish	elephant	moon	octopus	star

Find and circle the hidden pictures.

God created you in his image!

Bible Hidden Pictures

A Snake in the Garden

Genesis 3:4 and 5 tells us how the snake lied to Adam and Eve.

banana   grapes   leaf   snake   sun   tree

Find and circle the hidden pictures.

Jesus has forgiven everyone's sins!

2

Dry Land Ahead

Genesis 8:6–12 tells us how Noah sent a dove to find dry land.

| ark | cup | dove | mountain | rainbow | umbrella |

Find and circle the hidden pictures.

God takes care of you and me!

A Baby Brings Laughter

Genesis 21:1–7 tells us how happy Abraham and Sarah were when Isaac was born.

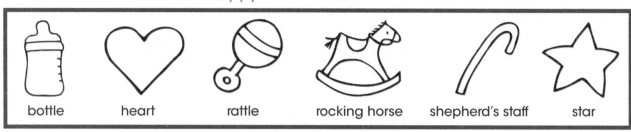

bottle heart rattle rocking horse shepherd's staff star

Find and circle the hidden pictures.

God rejoiced the day you were born!

Coat of Many Colors

Genesis 37:3 tells us how Joseph received a beautiful coat from his father.

Bible   chalice   coat   heart   pharaoh   shepherd's staff

Find and circle the hidden pictures.

Everyone is God's favorite!

Baby in a Basket

Exodus 2:5-6 tells us how baby Moses was found.

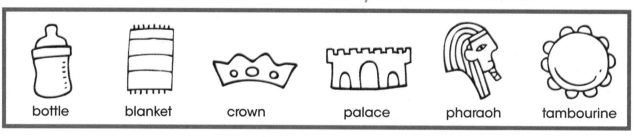

bottle   blanket   crown   palace   pharaoh   tambourine

Find and circle the hidden pictures.

God's love rescues you!

Crossing the Sea

Exodus 14:29–31 tells us how God led Moses across a sea.

| angel | chariot | donkey | fire | fish | tent |

Find and circle the hidden pictures.

God is with you wherever you go!

Bible Hidden Pictures

Tablets of Stone

Exodus 24:12 tells us how Moses received the Ten Commandments.

| idol | lightning bolt | mountain | sandals | snake | tablets |

Find and circle the hidden pictures.

Jesus commands you to love like he loves!

Walls Tumbled Down

Joshua 6:1–20 tells us how Jericho tumbled to the ground.

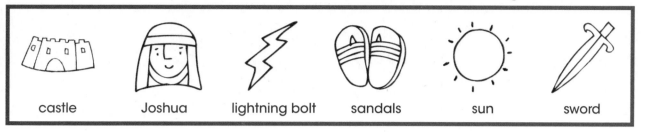

| castle | Joshua | lightning bolt | sandals | sun | sword |

Find and circle the hidden pictures.

God keeps his promises!

Bible Hidden Pictures

God Is Calling

1 Samuel 3:1–10 tells us how Samuel heard God call him three times.

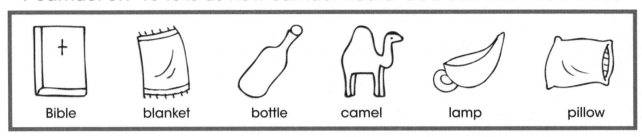

| Bible | blanket | bottle | camel | lamp | pillow |

Find and circle the hidden pictures.

God calls to you every day!

Bible Hidden Pictures   © School Zone Publishing Company 02120

A Boy and His Slingshot

1 Samuel 17 tells us how David defeated Goliath.

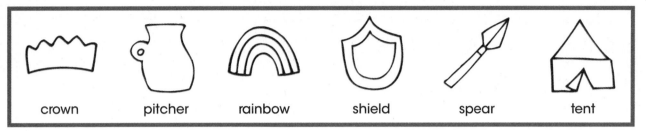

crown   pitcher   rainbow   shield   spear   tent

Find and circle the hidden pictures.

God wants you to be in his army!

Bible Hidden Pictures

Best Friends

1 Samuel 18:1 tells us how David and Jonathan became friends.

Bible   flute   lamb   King Saul   shepherd's staff   tree

Find and circle the hidden pictures.

God gives you friends to love!

Esther Is Queen

Esther 2:17 tells us how Esther was crowned queen.

| bottle | brush | crown | chalice | ring | King Xerxes |

Find and circle the hidden pictures.

You will receive a crown in heaven!

Flames of Fire

Daniel 3 tells us what three men survived the fiery furnace.

chalice   fire   idol   king   praying hands   steak

Find and circle the hidden pictures.

Everyone is safe in God's love!

The Lions' Den

Daniel 6:19–23 tells us how God kept Daniel safe.

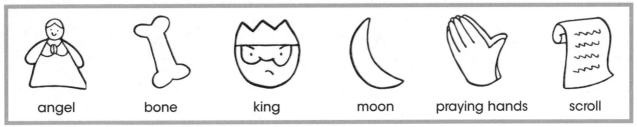

angel | bone | king | moon | praying hands | scroll

Find and circle the hidden pictures.

God listens when you pray!

Bible Hidden Pictures

A Big Fish

Jonah 1–2:10 tells us what happened to Jonah.

boat	city	crown	chalice	leaf	praying hands

Find and circle the hidden pictures.

God is with you wherever you are!

Bible Hidden Pictures · © School Zone Publishing Company 02120

Jesus Is Born

Luke 2:12 tells us where the shepherds found Jesus.

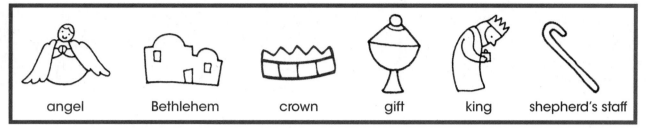

| angel | Bethlehem | crown | gift | king | shepherd's staff |

Find and circle the hidden pictures.

Hide God's word in your heart!

Jesus in the Temple

Luke 2:46 tells us where Jesus was when his parents found him.

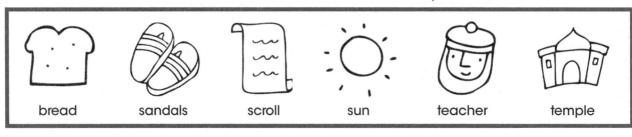

bread	sandals	scroll	sun	teacher	temple

Find and circle the hidden pictures.

You are never too young to share God's love!

Heaven Opened Up

Matthew 3:16–17 tells us how God spoke from heaven.

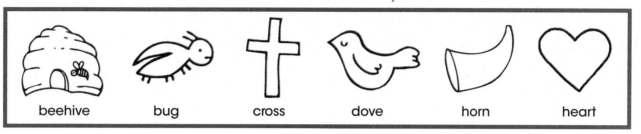

| beehive | bug | cross | dove | horn | heart |

Find and circle the hidden pictures.

Jesus baptizes you with the Holy Spirit!

Bible Hidden Pictures

Fishers of Men

Matthew 4:18–20 tells us how Jesus called his disciples.

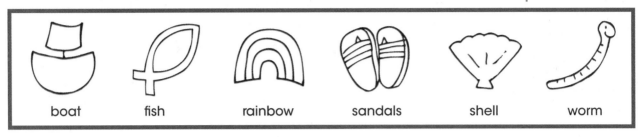

| boat | fish | rainbow | sandals | shell | worm |

Find and circle the hidden pictures.

You can be a disciple and follow Jesus!

Through the Roof

Mark 2:1–12 tells us how a roof was opened to see Jesus.

| Bible | house | key | mat | rope | saw |

Find and circle the hidden pictures.

your faith can help a friend!

Bible Hidden Pictures

Calming the Storm

Luke 8:22–25 tells us how a storm obeyed Jesus.

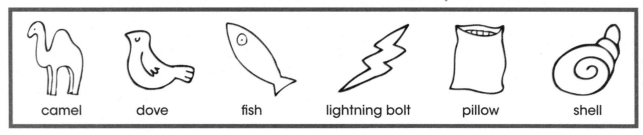

camel · dove · fish · lightning bolt · pillow · shell

Find and circle the hidden pictures.

Jesus is with you when you're afraid!

Bible Hidden Pictures   © School Zone Publishing Company 02120

Left by the Road

Luke 10:25–37 tells us about a Good Samaritan who helped his neighbor.

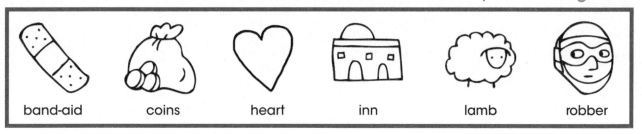

band-aid   coins   heart   inn   lamb   robber

Find and circle the hidden pictures.

Jesus wants you to help others!

Bible Hidden Pictures

Jesus Visits His Friends

Luke 10:38–42 tells us what Jesus said to Mary and Martha.

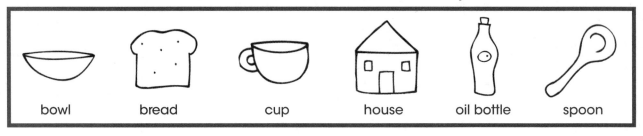

| bowl | bread | cup | house | oil bottle | spoon |

Find and circle the hidden pictures.

Take time for Jesus every day!

Bible Hidden Pictures

Walking on Water

Matthew 14:25–31 tells us how Jesus walked on water.

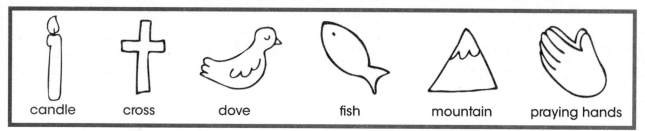

candle cross dove fish mountain praying hands

Find and circle the hidden pictures.

Never doubt God's love for you!

Bible Hidden Pictures

Lost Coin Found

Luke 15:8–10 tells us how a woman searched her house for a lost coin.

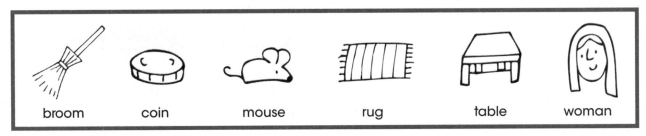

broom   coin   mouse   rug   table   woman

Find and circle the hidden pictures.

Jesus will find you wherever you are!

The Little Children

Mark 10:13–16 tells us what Jesus says about the kingdom of God.

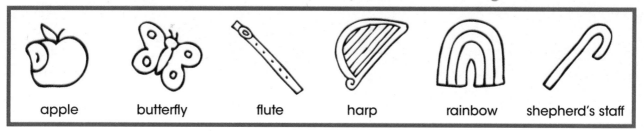

apple • butterfly • flute • harp • rainbow • shepherd's staff

Find and circle the hidden pictures.

Jesus loves you!

Bible Hidden Pictures

The Man in the Tree

Luke 19:1–10 tells us why Zacchaeus came out of the tree.

| cup | grapes | house | lamb | money | ruler |

Find and circle the hidden pictures.

Jesus loves everybody!

Bible Hidden Pictures   © School Zone Publishing Company 02120

Riding a Donkey

John 12:12-19 tells us the crowd shouted "Hosanna!" to Jesus.

blanket   cross   crown   donkey   horn   tunic

Find and circle the hidden pictures.

You can worship Jesus anytime!

     Bible Hidden Pictures

Jesus Died for All

Romans 6:10 tells us that Jesus died for everyone.

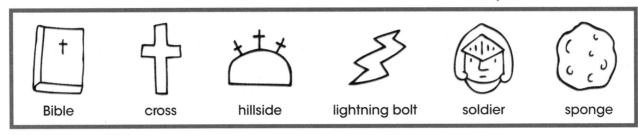

| Bible | cross | hillside | lightning bolt | soldier | sponge |

Find and circle the hidden pictures.

Jesus took away your sins!

The Empty Tomb

Mark 16:1-7 tells us what the women saw at the tomb.

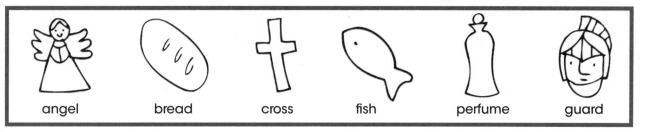

angel	bread	cross	fish	perfume	guard

Find and circle the hidden pictures.

You are alive with Jesus!

Bible Hidden Pictures

Flaming Spirit

Acts 2:3 tells us how the Holy Spirit came to the people.

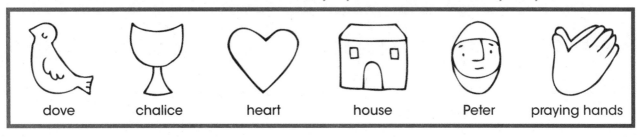

dove | chalice | heart | house | Peter | praying hands

Find and circle the hidden pictures.

Jesus promises to send the Holy Spirit to you!

Bible Hidden Pictures 02120